AFRICA'S SWEET CONNECTION

ALANA L. JOLLEY

ILLUSTRATED BY **PATTI MURPHY**

To order additional copies of this book, contact:
Xlibris
844-714-8691
www.Xlibris.com
Orders@Xlibris.com

ISBN: Softcover   978-1-4257-6870-6
         Hardcover   978-1-4257-6873-7
         EBook   978-1-6698-6075-4

Library of Congress Control Number: 2007906199

Print information available on the last page

Rev. date: 12/28/2022

for zion and eden

Prologue

Everybody knows that the sweet connection between people and bees has always been honey. But in Africa, honey has also been the sweet connection between people and a special bird called the honeyguide. The Borana tribe and the bird, honeyguide, worked together for centuries in the ancient tradition of collecting wild honey. Small boys, like Naseehu in this story, no longer learn about the honeyguide and its secrets because sugar now can be purchased in small stores close to most villages.

The Borana live in Southern Ethiopia and Kenya and speak a language called Oromifa. They are a segment of the largest tribe in Africa known as the Oromo. The Borana raise cattle and camels for a living; they are pastoralists. Their domed grass-hut villages, as well as their cattle, are moved from place to place according to seasons and location of water holes. The people are self-governed in a democratic system known as the Gadaa system where men and women are equal. They have their own special religion, and they pray to Waq, a god who "sends them all good things." Their clothing is simple: a shawl or a light blanket-type overwrap. Some women wear head coverings, and men sometimes wear prayer "beanies" or colorful blue turbans.

Wild honey is not as important to the Borana as it once was. However, they may still learn about the special tradition of honey collecting, thus keeping Africa's sweet connection alive for future generations.

AFRICA'S SWEET CONNECTION

by Alana L. Jolley

Naseehu tried to stay asleep, but he kept dreaming of bees buzzing around his head. He woke himself up swatting at them, and he had to feel his ears to see if they were still there. Around the campfire before going to sleep, his father, Jatani, and the elders told him stories about wild bees and a mysterious bird that guided people to bees' nests.

Long ago, the punishment for harming the bird was to cut off the ears. He wanted to learn about the bird, but he certainly did not want to lose his ears!

Naseehu knew daylight was approaching. He must be brave and start down the dusty path to meet his father. He grabbed his leather pouch, a big woven bag, and two wooden sticks, which he had placed by the platform of his bed. Silently, he left the hut where his mother and sisters were still asleep. He ran fast, past the thorn fences and cattle, past the sleeping camels, and past the sheep with their curly black faces. The huddled huts of his village disappeared behind him.

Jatani was not only Naseehu's father but also a Borana honey collector. Naseehu trusted his father, but still he was afraid to learn about the bird his grandfather had called Ngedde (in-getti). He knew if he learned the special bird ceremony well, he would someday take his father's place as a honey collector.

Bees and honey have been important to the Borana since ancient times. Naseehu thought of the stories about the faraway hills where steep cliffs held secrets

7

of the ancestors. His father told him about the pictures on the rocks and how, in bright sunlight, the shimmering images seemed to come alive. He secretly wished to meet those ancient artists, and he was thinking just that when he saw the shape of his own father flickering in the early dawn.

Walking side by side with Jatani, Naseehu was instructed once again how to summon the bird that would be their honeyguide. When they reached a clump of acacia trees, Naseehu took a small snail shell out of his pouch. He practiced blowing across it to make just the right sound that would attract the bird.

A high-pitched whistling sound came from the shell and pierced the stillness of the morning. At the same time, his father, Jatani, took the two wooden sticks and pounded up and down on the tree trunk. He continued pounding while making a trilling sound, *trrrr-trrrr*, with his tongue. In this way, Naseehu and his father worked together to attract the attention of a honeyguide that might be near. Naseehu was sure the bird would hear all the noise, no matter how far away it might be!

Suddenly, his father raised a hand to quiet the commotion. Naseehu heard a distant rattling sound. *Cutta-cutta-cutta.* High above his head, a small brown bird was circling. It flew away at first, then it came back.

Each time it circled, it repeated the same behavior; and each time, it came closer and closer.

Ngedde landed on a low branch, close enough for Naseehu to see under its wings. The bird was mostly brown on top, but underneath, its throat looked like a fluffy white cloud. The honeyguide started spreading and fluttering its wings excitedly, and then it began to chatter loudly.

"It is a female," his father whispered. "Ngedde only makes that kind of sound when she wants to guide."

The little brown bird kept arching her wings and fluttering her tail feathers. And she kept up the chattering. She abruptly darted upward, then circled back, and darted off again. Naseehu pointed to the sky and asked, "Does she want us to follow her?"

"Yes," replied Jatani, "but we have to hurry. Keep watching her, we don't want to lose her."

The honeyguide was easy to follow, even among the trees, as she kept repeating the same darting, circling, and chattering behavior over and over again. She made sure the two of them kept following her.

"The reason she guides people to beehives," his father told him, "is because her favorite food is beeswax and bee grubs (larvae)." Naseehu had learned that the bird eats mostly insects, but it likes beeswax better.

"How can she open a beehive with such a small beak?" Naseehu asked.

"Very good question," answered Jatani. "That's why she guides us to the bees' nests. Ngedde knows where all the beehives are in her territory, but she needs us to help her open a hive."

The two of them had been chasing the bird forever, it seemed to Naseehu, when Jatani once again raised his hand to be quiet and listen. Naseehu could hear a faint buzzing sound, which reminded him of his bad dreams. But where was the buzzing sound coming from? He didn't see any bees or any bees' nests. And the honeyguide was no longer circling and chattering, she just sat calmly on a tree branch. Now it was the bird's turn to watch the man and the boy. Jatani beckoned Naseehu to put his ear to a nearby tree trunk.

His father whispered, "She has not failed us. Quick! Build a fire and get the sticks. We must work fast!"

They held the long sticks over the fire
until the sticks were smoking. Then they began
hitting a tiny hole in the tree trunk. The hole
became wider and wider as they pounded, and
the buzzing got *louder* and *louder*.

Quickly, Jatani jabbed a smoking stick into the hole and pulled it out fast! Then, reaching in with a bare arm, he pulled out a great hunk of black honeycomb, dripping with thick golden honey.

Naseehu couldn't believe his eyes! How could his father do that? A swarm of angry bees charged out of the hive. He was sure his father would be stung a million times! But Jatani told him how the smoke from the stick calms the bees. He said, "A few bee stings are sometimes necessary in order to get the sweet reward."

Naseehu was so happy, so excited, and—oh—so very proud of what they had accomplished. But then he remembered his mother's warning words to him last night around the campfire.

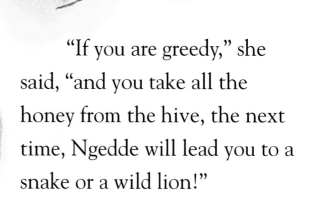

"If you are greedy," she said, "and you take all the honey from the hive, the next time, Ngedde will lead you to a snake or a wild lion!"

Naseehu thought this bird must really be special if you could lose your ears or be eaten by a wild animal if you do the wrong thing.

That's why it was so necessary for him to learn all these things from his father, the honey collector, and no one else. Naseehu placed a big piece of the honeycomb on a small branch lying on the ground. The little bird flew down and began feasting.

Most of the bees had left the hive, so the two honey collectors filled their sacks with just enough honeycomb for the village feast and the honey festival. Then they began their long walk home in

the desert heat. Naseehu now thought he felt bees buzzing in his stomach. He was so proud and happy to be returning to the village with his father. The people would be so happy.

As soon as they arrived, all the villagers gathered to greet them, poking and jabbing at their bodies and then at the big woven bag full of honeycomb. It was a great honor to share such success with all his kin.

He felt sure the ancestors were happy too because he would be able to carry on their ancient traditions. He wanted to run to those faraway cliffs to tell them that someday he would take his father's honored place as a honey collector among the Borana tribe.

Tomorrow, the women would make sweet treats, and they would mix the special honey drink for the festival and the great feast. Naseehu knew he would sleep well because his ears would stay in place, and his dreams would be sweet.

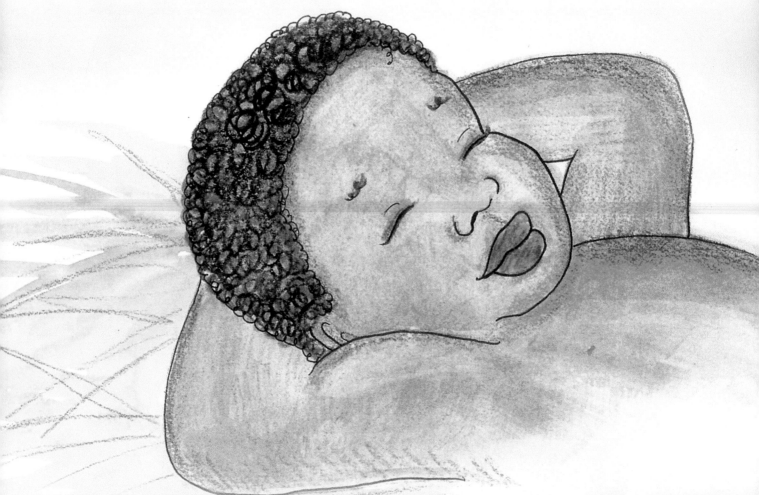

THE END

Printed in the United States
by Baker & Taylor Publisher Services